PRIVATE D

PRIVATE DOWDING

DOWDING

The personal story of a soldier killed in battle

With Notes by

WELLESLEY TUDOR POLE

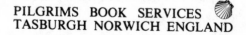

PILGRIMS BOOK SERVICES
TASBURGH NORWICH ENGLAND

First published August 1917
Second Edition September 1917
Third Edition November 1917
Fourth Edition October 1918
Fifth Edition January 1943
Sixth Edition 1966
Seventh Edition 1984

Printed by
The Thetford Press Ltd, Thetford, Norfolk

Somewhere within the soul there is silence.
Attain unto it. It is a pearl of great price.

Private Dowding.

CONTENTS

PREFACE TO THE SIXTH EDITION

SINCE the first appearance of this book, nearly half a century ago, many invaluable records have been published purporting to describe the conditions into which we pass when the time comes for us to leave this planet. To a certain extent 'Private Dowding' has proved to be a pioneer in this field.

This book has become a 'period piece' and should be read as such, although in my view the Message it contains was never more valuable than it is now.

Just as our experiences on earth are entirely individual and personal to each one of us, so it would seem are the experiences we meet as we pass forward into another world.

In spite of this fact it is to me both remarkable and significant that the majority of current writings on this important subject tend largely to confirm one another in their accounts of 'Borderland' conditions.

In regard to detail it should be remembered that no two people living through the same event, even here on earth, are able to describe or memorise it in the same way. It is natural, therefore that differences of perception and of outlook should colour the various accounts of what happens to us after 'death'.

This book contains a number of very optimistic predictions about the future welfare of the human race. A word of warning is necessary here. To those who live beyond the confines of time and space it is conceivable that a thousand years of human 'time' may appear to occupy the period of a single 'Day'.

I have no doubt that the prophecies given by the 'Messenger' in part III of this book are destined to be fulfilled long before our planet ceases to function as a living entity. Surely it is man's mission to do all in his power to bring the 'Golden Age' of which the 'Messenger' speaks, nearer than seems credibly possible to our restricted vision.

We should strive our utmost with this end in view, even if this end may seem remote and almost beyond the range of our present faith and understanding. We can take both courage and solace from the fact that a fresh spiritual Impulse is now making itself felt in our midst and that to our Creator, working through the hearts and minds of men, all things are not only possible but are certain to be harmoniously fulfilled in due course, both in time and in Eternity.

W.T.P.

Eastertide 1966.

INTRODUCTION

ON Monday, 12th March 1917, I was walking by the sea when I felt the presence of someone. I looked round; no one was in sight. All that day I felt as if someone were following me, trying to reach my thoughts. Suddenly I said to myself, 'It is a soldier. He has been killed in battle and wants to communicate!' That evening I happened to call upon a lady who possesses some degree of clairvoyant power. I had forgotten about the soldier, until she described a man dressed in khaki, sitting in a chair near me. He was gazing intently in my direction. She said he was mature, wore a small moustache, and seemed somewhat sad. Not a very intelligent character apparently, but an honest one. I came home and sat down at my writing-table. Immediately my pen moved. Did I move it? Yes, in an involuntary sort of way. The thoughts were not my own, the language was a little unusual. Ideas were mainly conveyed in short simple phrases. It would really seem as if some intelligence outside myself were speaking through my mind and my pen.

Some of the ideas are not in conformity with preconceived notions of my own.

The messages I received in this manner from 'Thomas Dowding,' recluse, schoolmaster, soldier, are set down exactly as they reached me.

Further comments on these messages will be found on pages 27, 39 and 78.

W.T.P.

BOURNEMOUTH,
  20th March 1917.

PART I

The Wilderness

One great truth has become my constant
companion. I sum it up thus: 'Empty yourself if you would be filled.'

Private Dowding.

12*th March* 1917, 9 p.m.

I AM grateful for this opportunity. You may not realise
how much some of us long to speak to those we have left
behind. It is not easy to get messages through with certainty.
They are so often lost in transit or misinterpreted. Sometimes the imagination of the receiver weaves a curious fabric
round the thoughts we try to pass down, then the ideas we
want to communicate are either lost or disfigured.

I was a schoolmaster ·in a small East Coast town before
the war. I was an orphan, somewhat of a recluse, and I
made friends but slowly. My name is of no importance;
apparently names over here are not needed. I became a
soldier in the autumn of 1915, and left my narrow village
life behind. These details, however, are really of no importance. They may act as a background to what I have to
say. I joined as a private and died as a private. My soldier-
ing lasted just nine months, eight of which were spent
training in Northumberland. I went out with my battalion
to France in July 1916, and we went into the trenches
almost at once. I was killed by a shell splinter one evening
in August, and I believe that my body was buried the following day. As you see, I hasten over these unimportant

13

events, important to me once, but now of no real consequence. How we overestimate the significance of earthly happenings! One only realises this when freed from earthly ties.

Well, my body soon became cannon fodder, and there were few to mourn me. It was not for me to play anything but an insignificant part in this world-tragedy, which is still unfolding.

I am still myself, a person of no importance; but I feel I should like to say a few things before passing along. I feared death, but then that was natural. I was timid, and even feared life and its pitfalls. So I was afraid of being killed and was sure it would mean extinction. There are still many who believe that. It is because extinction has not come to me that I want to speak to you. May I describe my experiences? Perhaps they may prove useful to some. How necessary that some of us should speak back across the border! The barriers must be broken down. This is one of the ways of doing it. Listen therefore to what I have to say:

Physical death is nothing. There really is no cause for fear. Some of my pals grieved for me. When I 'went West' they thought I was dead for good. This is what happened. I have a perfectly clear memory of the whole incident. I was waiting at the corner of a traverse to go on guard. It was a fine evening. I had no special intimation of danger, until I heard the whizz of a shell. Then followed an explosion, somewhere behind me. I crouched down involuntarily, but was too late. Something struck, hard, hard, hard, against my neck. Shall I ever lose the memory of that hardness? It is the only unpleasant incident that I can remember. I fell, and as I did so, without passing through any apparent interval of unconsciousness, I found myself outside myself! You see I am telling my story simply; you will find it easier to understand. You will learn to know what a small incident this dying is.

Think of it! One moment I was alive, in the earthly sense, looking over a trench parapet, unalarmed, normal. Five seconds later I was standing outside my body, helping two of my pals to carry my body down the trench labyrinth towards a dressing station. They thought I was senseless but alive. I did not know whether I had jumped out of my body through shell shock, temporarily or for ever. You see what a small thing is death, even the violent death of war! I seemed in a dream. I had dreamt that someone or something had knocked me down. Now I was dreaming that I was outside my body. Soon I should wake up and find myself in the traverse waiting to go on guard. . . . It all happened so simply. Death for me was a simple experience— no horror, no long-drawn suffering, no conflict. It comes to many in the same way. My pals need not fear death. Few of them do; nevertheless there *is* an underlying dread of possible extinction. I dreaded that; many soldiers do, but they rarely have time to think about such things. As in my case, thousands of soldiers pass over without knowing it. If there be shock, it is not the shock of physical death. Shock comes later when comprehension dawns: 'Where is my body? Surely I am not dead!' In my own case I knew nothing more than I have already related, at the time. When I found that my two pals could carry my body without my help, I dropped behind; I just followed, in a curiously humble way. Humble? Yes, because I seemed so useless. We met a stretcher party. My body was hoisted on to the stretcher. I wondered when I should get back into it again. You see, I was so little 'dead' that I imagined I was still (physically) alive. Think of it a moment before we pass on. I had been struck by a shell splinter. There was no pain. The life was knocked out of my body; again, I say, there was no pain. Then I found that the whole of myself—all, that is, that thinks and sees and feels and knows—was still alive and conscious! I had begun a new chapter of life. I will tell you what I felt like. It was as if I had been running hard until, hot and breathless, I had thrown my overcoat away. The coat was my body, and if I had not thrown it away I should have been suffocated. I cannot describe the experience in any better way; there is nothing else to describe.

My body went to the first dressing station, and after examination was taken to a mortuary. I stayed near it all that night, watching, but without thoughts. It was as if my being, feeling, and thinking had become 'suspended' by some Power outside myself. This sensation came over me gradually as the night advanced. I still expected to wake up in my body again—that is, so far as I expected anything. Then I lost consciousness and slept soundly.

No detail seems to have escaped me. When I awoke, my body had disappeared! How I hunted and hunted! It began to dawn upon me that something strange had happened, although I still felt I was in a dream and should soon awake. My body had been buried or burned, I never knew which. Soon I ceased hunting for it. Then the shock came! It came without any warning suddenly. I had been *killed* by a German shell! I was dead! I was no longer alive. I had been killed, killed, killed! Curious that I felt no shock when I was first driven outside my body. Now the shock came, and it was very real. I tried to think backwards, but my memory was numb. (It returned later.) How does it feel to be 'dead'? One can't explain, because there's nothing in it! I simply felt free and light. My being seemed to have expanded. These are mere words. I can only tell you just this: that death is nothing unseemly or shocking. So simple is the 'passing along' experience that it beggars description. Others may have other experiences to relate of a more complex nature. I don't know. . . .

When I lived in a physical body I never thought much about it. My health was fair. I knew very little about physiology. Now that I am living under other conditions I remain incurious as to that through which I express myself. By this I mean that I am still evidently in a body of some sort, but I can tell you very little about it. It has no interest for me. It is convenient, does not ache or tire, seems similar in formation to my old body. There IS a subtle difference, but I cannot attempt analysis.

Let me relate my first experience after I had somewhat recovered from the shock of realising I was 'dead'.

I was on, or rather above, the battlefield. It seemed as if I were floating in a mist that muffled sound and blurred the vision. Through this mist slowly penetrated a dim picture and some very low sounds. It was like looking through the wrong end of a telescope. Everything was distant, minute, misty, unreal. Guns were being fired. It might all have been millions of miles away. The detonation hardly reached me; I was conscious of the shells bursting without actually seeing them. The ground seemed very empty. No soldiers were visible. It was like looking down from above the clouds, yet that doesn't exactly express it either. When a shell that took life exploded, then the sensation of it came much nearer to me. The noise and tumult came over the border line *with* the lives of the slain. A curious way of putting it. All this time I was very lonely. I was conscious of none near me. I was neither in the world of matter nor could I be sure I was in any place at all! Just simply conscious of my own existence in a state of dream. I think I fell asleep for the second time, and long remained unconscious and in a dreamless condition.

At last I awoke. Then a new sensation came to me. It was as if I stood on a pinnacle, all that was essential of me. The rest receded, receded, receded. All appertaining to bodily life seemed to be dropping away down into a bottomless abyss. There was no feeling of irretrievable *loss*. My being seemed both minute and expansive at the same time. All that was not really me slipped down and away. The sense of loneliness deepened.

I do not find it easy to express myself. If the ideas are not clear, that is not your fault. You are setting down just what I impress upon you. How do I know this? I cannot see your pen, but I see my ideas as they are caught up and whirled into form within your mind. By 'form' perhaps I mean words. Others may not feel this loneliness. I cannot tell whether my experiences are common to many in a like position. When I first 'awoke' this second time, I felt cramped. This is passing and a sense of real freedom comes over me. A load has dropped away from me. I think my new faculties are now in working order. I can reason and think and feel and move.

Once I read a book about this after-life. It spoke of 'planes' and 'bodies' and 'cycles' and 'auras'. I think a man named Sinnett or Symons wrote it. It purported to deal with the history and geography of this after-life. I cannot confirm its descriptions from my own experience. I am simply myself, alive, in a region where food and drink seem unnecessary. Otherwise 'life' is strangely similar to earth life. A 'continuation', but with more freedom. I have no more to say just now. Will you let me return another time and use your mind again? I shall be so grateful.

13th March 1917, 8 p.m.

You are kind to me. You loan me a power I do not possess any longer—the power to convey information to my human fellows on earth.

I can use your mind freely because I see you have deliberately chained your imagination, and so I can impress you freely and clearly.

From this you may notice that I am a little further along my new road. I have been helped. Also I have recovered from the 'shock', not of my transition but of my *recognition* of it. This is no subtilty, it is simply what I mean. I am no longer alone—I have met my dear brother. He came out here three years ago and has come down to welcome me. The tie between us is strong. William could not get near me for a long time, he says. The atmosphere was so thick. He hoped to reach me in time to avert the 'shock' to which I have referred, but found it impossible.

He is working among the newly arrived and has wide experience.

A good deal of what follows came to me from him; I have made it my own, and so can pass it on. You see, I am still possessed with the desire to make my experience, my adventure, of help to others who have not yet arrived here. It appears that there are Rest Halls in this region, specially prepared for newly arrived pilgrims. I shall use your language. We can only convey our experiences *approximately*. To describe conditions here in WORDS is quite impossible. Please remember this. My brother helped me into one of these Rest Halls. Confusion at once dropped away from me. Never shall I forget my happiness. I sat in the alcove of a splendid domed hall. The splashing of a fountain reached my tired being and soothed me. The fountain 'played' music, colour, harmony, bliss. All discordancies vanished and I was at peace. My brother sat near me. He could not stay long, but promised to return. I wanted to find you at once to tell you I had found peace, but it is only now that I could do so. On earth, the study of crystal formations was a great hobby of mine. To my intense delight I discovered that this splendid hall was constructed according to the law of crystal formations. I spent hours in examining various parts of it. I shall spend hours and days and weeks here. I can continue my studies and make endless discoveries. What happiness! When I have regained a state of poise, my brother says I may help him in his work outside. I am in no hurry for this.

You evidently know nothing about crystals. I cannot impress your mind with the wonders of this place. What a pity! This place is so different from any earthly edifice that I fear it is useless to attempt description. As it is, people will say I am romancing. Or else they will say that you, my faithful scribe, have let your imagination run away with you. Please let me return again later. I still have much to say.

14*th March* 1917, 5 p.m.

I am beginning to meet people and to exchange ideas.
Strange that the only person I came across for a long time
was my brother. He tells me that I have never been really
alone. The mist around me, shutting me off, has emanated
from myself, he says. This fact rather humiliates me. I suppose my loneliness of life and character whilst on earth
have followed me here. I always lived in books, they were
my real world. And even then, my reading was technical
rather than general.

I begin to see now that my type of mind would find
itself isolated, or rather would emanate isolation, when
loosed from earthly trammels. I shall remain near earth
conditions whilst learning lessons I refused to learn
before.

It is dangerous to live *to and for oneself*. Tell this to my
fellows with emphasis. The life of a recluse is unwise, except for the very few who have special work that requires
complete silence and isolation. I was not one of these. I
cannot remember doing anything really worth while. I never
looked outside myself.

My school? Well, teaching bored me. I simply did it to
earn my bread and cheese. People will say I was unique,
a crabby, selfish old bachelor. Selfish yes, but alas!
far from being unique. I was thirty-seven when I came over
here—that is, my body was. Now I feel so ignorant and
humble that I don't feel I've begun to have any age
at all.

I must dwell on this. Live widely. Don't get isolated. Exchange thoughts and services. Don't read too much.
That was my mistake. Books appealed to me more than

life or people. I am now suffering for my mistakes. In
passing on these details of my life I am helping to free
myself.

What a good thing the war dragged me out into life!
In those nine months I learned more about human nature
than I had conceived possible. Now I am learning about
my poor fossilized old self. It is a blessing I came here.
Though I do not regret, I like to hear what is going on in
the region you inhabit. It seems a long way off already. I
told my brother I wanted news about events on earth. He
took me to visit an old gentleman who had been editor
of a newspaper. Why did I call him 'old'? Because he died
at eighty-one and has not thrown off earth conditions yet.
He therefore surrounds himself with these conditions. His
son on earth runs the paper, a French journal. The old man
can read his son's thoughts and so divines the world's news
through his son's mind. He has built himself an office, full
of telephones and tape machines. These machines are in a
way illusory, but they please the old gentleman. He received
me courteously, and insisted on hearing details of my crossing. He was disappointed that I did not know his paper
by name or reputation, and surprised that I knew so little
about earthly affairs. 'I want to get back. I cannot get along
without my paper. My son often uses my ideas in his
editorials without knowing it.' This fact was the cause of
much amusement to him. I asked him for some current
news. This is what he told me:

'Something interesting is going on, for my son stays at
the office all night. There is "war as usual". There is some
commotion about food. I saw Guilbert writing an article
for the paper on "World Shortage". England seems to be

scared about it. They have suddenly remembered the existence of the land they are fighting for, and they are digging
it about. Something must have stopped food supplies or
destroyed them.

'Food seems more important now than shells. The rest
of the world seems coming into the war—at least, Guilbert
thinks so.

'I see an article headed "America and China". Are they
short of food too, or are they to fight? I think they are
going to side with France. Turkey must be having a bad
time. I see the headlines "Turkish Débâcle". Guilbert seems
full of excitement about Russia. I see into his mind. He is
evolving an article on "Russia: the Coming World Power".
Russia must have won a big victory somewhere. Yes, I
think the war is going on all right. Our circulation has in-
creased again, but, alas! Guilbert cannot get enough paper.
I wish I were down there. I would have laid in a big stock
months ago.'

The old gentleman was still rambling on about his paper
and its prospects when I came away. How awful to be
chained to an earthly property like that! Tell people to control their worldly interests *from outside*. If you identify
yourself heart and soul with some material project or
undertaking, you will find it hanging on to you over here.
It will obsess you, blot out the view, make progress impossible. This old French editor came over a good many years
ago. He still lives on earth in mind, so far as he is allowed
to do so. Take a bird's-eye, dispassionate view of all your
worldly interests. Master them or they will master you. In
the latter case, when you get here you will be miserable.
Life will seem empty, a wilderness. Earth ties will tighten

their grip, yet you will be unable to respond. Confusion will result—that is purgatory.

There are many forms. Each of us creates his own purgatorial conditions. If I had my time over again how differently I should live my life! I was not one of those who lived only for the purpose of satisfying ambition. Money was a secondary consideration. Yes, I erred at the other extreme, for I neither lived enough among my fellow-men nor interested myself sufficiently in their affairs. Well, I have created my own purgatory. I must live through it somehow. Good night. I will return again.

14th March 1917, 8 p.m.

I want to tell you what I have been doing. On returning to my alcove in the Rest Hall I found someone else there.

He told me he was a messenger from another sphere, higher up. Certainly wisdom shone from his eyes. I think he had just come in for a little quiet. I made as if to go away, but he beckoned me back. 'You are speaking to earth. Do not hurry to describe your new life and surroundings. Take my advice: do a little living first. . . .' I think he saw surprise in my face. 'Do you know,' he continued, 'that most of what you have conveyed to your friend at the matter end of the line is quite illusory?' 'What do you mean?' I cried. 'You will gradually find out for yourself. Remember what I have just said.' This conversation has perturbed me. I try to dismiss it from my mind, but it sticks. It makes me feel smaller still. Am I really the fool rushing in where angels fear to tread? After all, what do I know about my present life? I have not mastered the natural laws of this place. I have not even mastered myself. I remember meeting a man in a railway train when I was a young student in London.

He was full of the theory that all 'phenomenal' life, as he termed it, was merely illusion. He called it 'māya'. I thought the fellow mad. He said he had read up the whole subject at the British Museum. How I scoffed! Now that I come to look back upon my 'phenomenal' life on earth, I begin to see that it consisted mainly of 'māya'! A long chain of illusory episodes with my poor little self in the centre. Was there anything *permanent* in the earth conditions through which I passed during my thirty-seven years? I begin to think not. That idea does not worry me any longer. My past illusions may be buried out of sight with my body, for all I care.

I don't like to think that my impressions about myself and my *present life* are mere illusions too! That rankles. It humiliates. Unfortunately, I fear it may be true. I have given the matter much thought. Evidently I am in a state of consciousness not far removed from earthly existence. I am journeying towards a wider, truer life, but I am not yet there. I have no right to speak with any authority of my experiences here. I am ashamed of having troubled you. One thought consoles me. If this really *is* a state of illusion, or illusory ideas, in which I find myself— well, others must pass through it too. Perhaps the ideas I have tried to express may help some of those who are not yet here. Anyway, my life seems quite as real as it did on earth, even more real. There is *something* that lives and moves within me that is *not* illusion. That something will forge its way out into the light some day. I can but go on trying. Meanwhile perhaps I had better not come to you again. Let me thank you for your patience. You have helped me through difficult purgatorial hours. I may return. I do not know. Meanwhile * * * Good night.

PART II

The Awakening

If you would dwell in peace, learn to love deeply.

Private Dowding

I HARDLY expected to hear from my soldier friend again. I had asked him previously why he enlisted so early in the war. He told me he was tired of being a schoolmaster, and the war fever would not leave him alone. Never have I met anyone less like a soldier! The poor man must have endured much hardship during his training, owing to his very sensitive and retiring disposition. He had told me that in earth life he was a little short-sighted, prematurely grey at thirty-six, and that he walked with a stoop. One wonders how he came to be accepted in those early days of the war, when so much fine physical material was available. He was evidently a scholar in his way; apparently well read in science and mathematics. All his acquired learning seems to have dropped from him at 'death', and he becomes a little child groping his way amidst strange surroundings; lonely, bewildered. It is not easy to believe that I have imagined the whole of this experience; that Private Dowding is a figment without reality. This explanation is possible. I do not wish to brush it aside lightly, but it does not appeal to me. I can but record the experience as it came to me, and let my readers judge.

I now set down the next series of notes exactly as they reached me.

W.T.P.

16th March 1917, 5 p.m.

You will be surprised. I did not expect to speak to you again. I will tell you how it has come about.

I have met the 'Messenger' again. I fancy he was looking for me. He wanted to know how I was getting on. I told him I had broken off communication with my earth friend, on his advice. He said he had been speaking to my brother and had learnt my history. My brother had told him how much consolation I derived from speaking to you. He then said that perhaps he had spoken a little hastily, without full knowledge of the facts. He did not think there would be much harm if I kept the channel open a little longer. He impressed on me the importance of reminding you that the conditions now around me are impermanent, and, to that extent, unreal. From his standpoint, the value of such messages as these depended upon the emphasis placed on this fact. The spiritual world is everywhere. The life of spirit is eternal, perfect, supreme. We humans hide from the light. We grovel among the illusions created by our thoughts. We surround ourselves with misconceptions. We refuse to rise into the Christ Sphere. The Christ Sphere is everywhere, and yet, by some strange paradox, we were able to shut it out from view. All these thoughts were new to me. I begin to see what is meant. If I did not do so, I could not pass the ideas on. You say these thoughts are quite familiar to you. I am surprised at this. What a little world I have been living in!

This Messenger evidently came from the Christ Sphere. Religion never meant much to me. Now I begin to see that one cannot live without it.

A great deal was said about reflection: how we can clear

out our own poor thoughts and illusions and allow the Christ power to reflect through us. Evidently this power is wonderful. The Messenger seemed to love to speak of it; yet he was in awe of it. It clears away illusions as the sun .clears away fog. He said I am still living in a fog, a fog of my own creation and design. Well! Well! Once I thought I knew a lot. Then I was sure I knew a little. Now I know I know nothing. It appears that the war is based upon an illusion. I wonder what my old Parisian friend would say to that! Since the Great War began, I believe people have thought it was the only reality on earth! Now I am told it is all based on—illusion. I am told that lust for wealth (of one material kind or another) was the real cause of the war. Neverthless, as a result of the war, all the nations engaged will be far poorer than they were before.

This idea had not crossed my mind. I was told another thing. Your war down there is being turned into a celestial instrument. It was put to me like this. Material forces are becoming exhausted—that is to say, the more they are used the less they achieve. Strange thought! People will realise that material force leads nowhere, is indeed an illusion. I cannot quite grasp the idea yet.

Apparently the impotent clash of conflicting material forces is creating a kind of vacuum. The Messenger said this fact implied a supreme mystery. Into this vacuum spiritual power is to be poured and poured. He had seen with his own eyes the Reservoirs. He spoke of these Reservoirs with bated breath. The light of Heaven is reflected in them. The Water of Life fills them. This Life is still beyond our conception. Our human life is but a shadow. High beings, God's messengers, guard the sluice gates. They await the Word of command. Then will the Water of Life be released.

Already it is available to many. Do you remember that passage in Revelation about the river of the Water of Life, bright as crystal, proceeding from God?

The Messenger told me that we are entering into the period of revelations, when all prophecies will be fulfilled. These things are beyond me. While he was speaking, I felt as if I were suspended in space, without visible support. Those high and holy matters are of a spiritual nature. They do not belong to the realms of illusion. I cannot attain to such ideas. I hardly dare to contemplate them. I pass them on because I believe they may justify me in keeping the channel open between us. If I only report matters that interest me, connected with my present illusory surroundings, the avenue between us will close up. We cannot live on the celestial heights until we have completed our work in the valleys. That is how I feel. A friend of mine once tried to climb Mont Blanc. He turned back long before the summit was reached. He could not breath in the rarefied atmosphere. The guides and the rest of the party went on. Alas that I should be one of those forced 'to turn back'. I never used my opportunities during earth life. My spiritual nature atrophied. You must excuse this self-analysis. . . . How wonderful it must be to be among those who never turn back! God willing, I will begin to climb. God willing, I too will never turn back! God willing, the whole human race will never turn back, now it has begun to climb. The Messenger said that a cycle was ending, that human life had just entered an upward arc. This conveys very little to me, but I pass it on. . . . I am sad. I am worth so little. I will come again.

16th March 1917, 8 p.m.

When I left off speaking to you, my brother came up. He said I needed rest. He blamed the Messenger for telling me more than I could stand or understand. William took me to a Hall of Silence. I had never been there before. Heaven's dome was above me. The silence of the spheres surrounded me. The loneliness of the desert was my only companion. There I seemed to remain a very long time, but time also is an illusion. The meaning behind this word still rouses conflicting emotions within me. Shall I be for ever the slave of my own illusions? It is impossible to tell. I shall visit the Hall of Silence regularly. Strength and consolation came to me within its walls. All that the Messenger had said came back to me. Understanding of many truths dawned within me. One great truth has become my constant companion. I sum it up thus: 'Empty yourself if you would be filled.' The Waters of Life can never flow through me until I have surrendered my whole self. I begin to see the wisdom of this. To you it may convey nothing. I have begun to try to pour myself away. It is a strange experience. Jesus talked of the children. They entered heaven. The gateway was barred to the wise men. Children have little to unlearn. Although I know nothing, yet have I much to unlearn. This is indeed a paradox.

I believe this Hall of Silence is available to you also. Try to find the road that leads there. War roars through your lives. The thunder of it is everywhere. I am still unable to shut out its rumbling completely. Somewhere within the soul there is silence. Attain unto it. It is a pearl of great price. I speak of what I know. I do not think the importance of silence is dwelt upon sufficiently in the Christian scriptures. I never remember being taught its vast import when on earth. I begin to realise what is meant by the Still small voice of God! I am now more myself. My brother has offered to let me help him in his work: I am glad. Good night.

17th March 1917, 5 p.m.

I have looked into hell! I may have to return to that region. I shall be given my choice. Grant that I may be strong enough to offer myself freely. Hell is a thought region. Evil dwells there and works out its purposes. The forces used to hold mankind down in the darkness of ignorance are generated in hell! It is not a place; it is a condition. The human race has created the condition. It has taken millions of years to reach its present state. I dare not tell you what I saw there. My brother needed help. A soldier had been killed who had committed very evil deeds. I will draw a veil over them. He was a degenerate, a murderer, a sensualist. He died cursing God and man. An awful death. This man was drawn towards hell by the law of attraction. My brother had been told off to rescue him. He took me with him. At first I refused to go. Then I went. . . . An angel of light came to protect us, otherwise we should have been lost in the blackness of the pit. This sounds sensational, even grotesque. It is the truth.

The power of evil! Have you any idea of its mighty strength, its lure? Can that power be an illusion too? The angel said so. The angel said the power of hell was now at its supreme height. It drew its power from man! As man rose toward spiritual life the powers of darkness would subside and finally become extinguished. 'Extinguished' is my word. The angel said 'transmuted'. That conception is

quite beyond me. We descended gloomy avenues. The darkness grew. There was a strange allurement about the atmosphere. Even the angel's light grew dim. I thought we were
lost. At moments I *hoped* we were lost. So strong is the
attraction. I cannot understand it. Something sensual within me leaped and burned. I thought I had emptied myself
of self before undertaking this great adventure. Had I done
so, I should have been safe. As it was, I should have been
lost but for the angel's and my brother's help. I felt the
giant lusts of the human race. They thrilled through me. I
could not keep them out. We descended deeper. I say 'descended'. If hell is not a place, how can one 'descend'? I
asked my brother. He said we were not moving in the physical sense. Our progress depended on certain thought processes evoked by the Will.

It is all very strange to me. I now remember that the
Messenger told me I was *not* to dwell on what I saw and
felt in this dark region. Therefore I will hurry on and not
dwell upon details. As a matter of fact, I never reached
the point where the rescue was attempted. The angel and
my brother went alone. I waited for their return in what
seemed to be a deep dark forest. There was no life, no light
there. One felt stagnation everywhere. The angel said that
was the most insidious kind of hell, stagnation, because no
one recognised it as such. Contrary to belief, hell itself, or
rather that part of it visited by my brother and the angel,
is brilliantly lighted.

The light is coarse, artificial. It keeps out the light of
God. In this awful glare the angel's light nearly lost its
radiance.

All this my brother told me afterwards. Those who die

filled with thoughts of selfishness and sensuality are at-
tracted down the grey avenues toward this hell of the senses.
The darkness of the deep forests appals, the loneliness is
intense. At last, light is seen ahead. It is not the light of
heaven, it is the lure of hell. These poor souls hasten onwards, though not toward destruction; there is no such
thing. They hasten down into conditions that are the
counterpart of their own interior condition. The Law is at
work. This hell is a hell of the illusions and is itself an
illusion. I find this hard to credit. Those who enter it are
led to believe that the only realities are the sense passions
and the beliefs of the human 'I'. This hell consists in believ-
ing the unreal to be real. It consists in the lure of the senses
without the possibility of gratifying them. I was told a
great deal more about this awful region, but I must not
pass it on. The angel said that the 'condition' would ultimately dissolve into nothingness. Hell, apparently, or that
part of it we are speaking about, depends for its existence
on human thoughts and feelings. The race will never rise to
greatness until the passions are controlled. This refers to
nations and to individuals. On earth I was never interested
in such matters. I did not realise the existence of the sexual
canker at the heart of human life. What a terrible thing this
is! Do not wait until you come over here. Set to work at
once. There is no time to lose. Gain control of self. Then
retain control by emptying yourself of self. All the thoughts
of lust and passion, greed, hatred, envy, and, above all,
selfishness, passing through the minds of men and women,
generate the 'condition' called hell. Purgatory and hell are
different states. We all must needs pass through a purging,
purifying process after leaving earth life. I am still in purgatory. Some day I shall rise above it. The majority who come

over here rise above or rather THROUGH purgatory into
higher conditions. A minority refuse to relinquish their
thoughts and beliefs in the pleasures of sin and the reality
of the sense life. They sink by the weight of their own
thoughts. No outside power can attract a man against his
will. A man sinks or rises through the action of a spiritual
law of gravity. He is never safe until he has emptied himself completely. You see how I emphasise this fact. Some
of these thoughts came to me whilst I waited in the gloomy
forest. Then the angel and my brother returned. They had
found him for whom they sought. He would not come away.
They had to leave him there. Fear held him. He said his
existence was awful, but he was afraid to move for fear
worse conditions befell.

Fear chained him. No outside power can unchain that
man. Release will come from within some day. Sadly we
returned to our own places. I began to realise what power
King Fear holds over nearly all of us. The angel said that
Fear would be destroyed when Love came into her own.
He said the time was coming. . . . I have much to think
about. I am going into the Hall of Silence. If I can return
again, I will. Good bye.

                                    17th March 1917, 8 p.m.
Soon after returning from the states of hell I met the
messenger again. He said I had not learned sufficient of the
spiritual life to visit such dark regions with impunity. He
took me with him toward a Mount of Vision. The light
was dazzling. No doubt he thought such a pilgrimage would
prove an antidote to my journey toward the demon realm.
It was almost too much for me. I can remember little of
what I saw. I gazed upon the Reservoirs of Illumination.

They were afar off. They nearly blinded me. The Messenger told me many things concerning the manifestations of God to man. He said a prophet of the Most High was in charge of each of the gateways to those Reservoirs of Light. When darkness and ignorance grew apace among men, the 'Word' was uttered. Then the prophet, whose turn it was to descend among men, made deep obeisance and opened wide his own gateway to the Reservoirs of Light. He descended to earthly regions that he might guide the spreading of the new illumination. The Messenger told me that one of these holy prophets fulfilled his divine mission during the last century. He said the illumination then released was about to spread through East and West. The prophet has returned to heavenly spheres—his work accomplished. His work would become manifest when the war was over. The war itself was an outward manifestation of the powers of evil in their attempt to obstruct the inflow of light. It was very interesting, but beyond me. He said a spiritual revival was destined to take place within all the great world-faiths.

He said that unity would become established, that universal peace would become an accomplished fact. He seemed to imply that the golden era was at hand; nearer indeed than we could realise. He asked me to return to the Mount of Vision with him, but I feel I cannot, dare not do so. I am unworthy. I cannot unself myself sufficiently. Such heights are not for such as I am! I returned to my own place alone, by the force of an interior gravity. But I ask you to mark the Messenger's words. He spoke of what he knew. Let his words blaze forth a channel through the minds of men.

I ask this of you: to make them known.

I have returned once more.

There are several things I want to say. I find it difficult to tell you what they are.

I will tell you why. I am a person who cannot pretend to teach or preach. I do not wish to do so. I am not sure enough of my own faith yet.

I feel it my duty to tell you something of what the angel and the Messenger said, not because I understand or believe it all, but because they have been good to me. They have recognised my ignorance, have not scoffed at my unworthiness. I have not come to you to preach, to show the way to heavenly states. I do not know my way there, so how could I guide you? You are probably nearer heaven than I, though still on earth. Because I pass on what has been told to me, do not think I am a 'superior' person. Do not think that all I say must be true. It may be. I cannot tell myself. I am grateful to you for listening to me. I am grateful to my brother for meeting me over here. Above all, I thank God for the Messenger who deigns to come and talk to me at intervals. I have met other people over here, and have been allowed to help one or two distressed souls. But I remain a lonely person, working out my own salvation in fear and trembling. Put fear behind you! That is one of the things I must say—I try to do it. Fear is a power opposed to life; it is the weapon of the Evil One. It is illusion. Can you believe what I say? Fear has no reality of its own. Its power is generated from within ourselves. Cast it out. Never fear again.

I want to say a few words about love—very few, because I know so little. Also because love is spoken about too much already, whereas it should be lived. If you would dwell in peace, learn to love deeply. Never cease from loving. Jesus said a good deal about love, if I remember rightly. Look up what He said and *live it*.

Love God by pouring yourself away. Love your fellows by giving them all you possess of light and truth.

Love LOVE for her own blessed sake. Such love will bring you nearer heaven.

I have spoken about illusion several times. I return to it once more. I begin to see that phenomenal existence, whether on earth or here, is so impermanent as to be unreal. This is a hard saying. I do not yet understand it.

Live above those conditions which, after much meditation, appear to you to be illusory. That is the best advice I can give.

The Messenger has spoken several times about evil. I cannot entirely shake off the effects of my visit to the lower regions, where evil reigns as lord and king.

It appears that evil is not real or permanent. Its *power* is permanent, but this power can be transmuted, until it serves ends that are divine. More than this I cannot say, because I do not know. If you can realise that evil has no real existence and can be eliminated entirely from human life, you will have learnt much. Remember what was said about stagnation. Keep moving in some direction all the time. How was it that I lived so stagnantly whilst on earth?—Let my life be an example.

One other thought I wish to leave with you. The Messenger told me that we have entered the period of revelations. The childhood of the race is nearly over. Vast spiritual purifying powers are waiting to be poured forth. Create vessels for this purpose! Make yourself a vessel that you may receive the gift of the Spirit. You will then require no teaching from outside. Revelation will come to you from within. Retire into the Hall of Silence. Think on these things. Think on these things. . . . The time has come for my withdrawal. I will ask the Messenger to bless your life and work. You are a soldier too. Your life will bring you many opportunities. You will be protected, safeguarded, illumined. Should it be your fate to come across to this region soon, I will try to meet you. I may be useful. But I do not think you are coming yet. I have said so much about myself! Only now, as I am leaving, do I speak of you. Forgive me. Once more, my friend, I thank you. I owe you more than I can repay. In some special manner you have buoyed up my faith when it would have failed me otherwise. God grant you understanding. God grant you peace.

Note by W.T.P.

I have not heard again from my friend. He has evidently passed beyond my ken. Probably he is already free from earth conditions and has entered upon the pilgrimage of selfless service.

I can quite believe that this is possible. His nature was *au fond* humble and childlike. The humility of the man was indeed very splendid. I hope we may meet again some day.

There are several points in his narrative worthy of comment. I must treat the whole experience as real. Otherwise it would not have been worth while setting down. To me,

my communications with Thomas Dowding were so real that
he seemed to be in the room sitting at my elbow, prompting
my pen. I know there have been many books written con-
taining messages, said to have been passed down from another plane of existence. One cannot doubt the possibility
of 'spirit communion', as it is often called. It seems to me
that there can be no final proof concerning these matters.
One must be guided by the interior worth of the messages
themselves. I tell you, for instance, that I am satisfied I have
been speaking with a soldier who was killed in battle seven
months ago. I have set down the experience in writing exactly as it came to me. I cannot, however, prove the genuineness of the experience to anyone else. I cannot even prove
it finally to myself.

I will now comment upon Thomas Dowding's statements
and beliefs, in the search for interior evidences of their
genuineness. It is evident that these messages come from a
mind in a state of consciousness not far removed from
earthly existence, and not from any more spiritual source.
I believe that the messages set down in a little book called
Christ in You were received inspirationally in a manner
akin to the experiences with which we are now dealing. The
interior evidence of the *Christ in You* communication certainly points to their being genuine. The spirit of truth
breathes from these pages, and therefore their actual source
is a matter of little moment. Can the same be said of the
messages from Thomas Dowding? They belong to a
different order of communication and must be considered in
the light of their own internal worth.

In the first place, Dowding, or whoever is speaking, has
no very clear idea of what truth is. He emphasises the fact
that he knows nothing. He passes on the information he

receives from the 'Messenger' and the 'angel', but he cannot very often endorse the truth of such information in the
light of his own experience. In one place, he says he is
helping to 'free himself' (presumably from ignorance) by
passing on the details of his life. As the record proceeds,
one is forced to the conclusion that our friend finds the
shackles dropping from him. The tone of his remarks begins to change. A new and more spiritual note becomes
apparent. He takes more interest in what the Messenger
tells him.

He realises more and more the worthlessness of human
'knowledge', and proceeds to empty his mind, that it may
begin to reflect spiritual rather than earthly ideas. In a
way, his humility and his confidence grow together, yet a
certain diffidence is noticeable right to the end.

One does not know why he felt impelled to communicate
with earth, nor why he chose to 'speak' to one who was an
entire stranger to him. He does not seem to think that doubt
will be cast upon his story; indeed, he goes out of his way
to say that my imagination has been 'chained', and that
his ideas are correctly taken down. The Messenger warns
our friend against communicating with earth at all.
'Do you know that most of what you have conveyed
to your friend at the matter end of the line is quite
illusory?' This is a very perturbing thought to Private
Dowding, but he is told that he will gradually discover
the truth of what the Messenger tells him. Towards
the end he does begin to disentangle that which is real in
his life from the unreal, and does his best to tell us how he
reaches his conclusions. On this point his final dictum is
this: 'Live above all those conditions that appear to you,
after much meditation, to be illusory.' He is forced to the

conclusion that very little of his own earth life or of his present life can be termed 'real' in any final sense. Nevertheless, his faith in a spiritual life gradually grows, until he is able to exclaim: 'There is *something* that lives and moves in me that is *not* illusion. That something will forge its way out into the light some day.'

It will be noted that I have called my friend Thomas Dowding. It is very difficult to get through names correctly. Dowding may have been our friend's earth label, but I doubt if it is a matter of any importance. The only name he himself mentions is that of William, belonging to his brother, who meets him on the 'other side'. Names are evidently of no moment over there.

Finally, let me say a few words on the teaching that comes to our friend as he wanders about seeking for truth. To my mind, there is much of value and real beauty in the spiritual lessons conveyed to him by the personage he calls the 'Messenger'. Evidently only fragments of these messages have been passed on to us. I think our friend was unable to grasp the import of a great deal he was told, and feared to pass it on. Evidently he originates no teaching himself and is careful to point this out. He says: 'I cannot pretend to preach or teach. . . . I am not sure of my own faith yet.' Then he goes on to explain why he feels it his duty to pass on the teaching of the angel and the Messenger. Personally, I consider that this teaching, whatever its actual source may be, is well worth careful attention and study. It certainly does not emanate from my own mind, conscious or subconscious—that is, so far as one is in a position to judge. I realise that the mysteries of the subliminal and subconscious regions are still beyond our grasp.

Because of this, I say, study the teaching itself. Accept

or reject it according to its own interior worth. Again and again I would urge the importance of studying the teaching in its relation to life as we now know it. Except in that aspect, no such communication from the other side can have any practical value.

Do not confuse the teaching with the simple record of Private Dowding's surroundings. He tells us that from the standpoint of the Messenger the value of the messages depends upon the emphasis placed upon the fact of the impermanence of the conditions described, and it must never be forgotten, if the teaching in this narrative seems incomplete, that Private Dowding does not pretend to teach. He himself is still seeking, and that somewhat blindly. He says he knows nothing. His was not an enlightened soul. He passes on fragments of a teaching which he only dimly understands, and the value of these fragments to us must lie in our reading of their deeper meaning in relation to our own lives.

If his loneliness is not at first understood, we have to bear in mind that he made no profession of faith here, and consequently his vision of higher things must have been very dim on crossing over. It may be that all those who are without an appreciation of inner values, are, in a sense, in the same spiritual loneliness, shut off as they are from the perfect inviolable whole 'by the fragmentary bodily senses, and by the limitations of the sense-intellect— that is to say, by the intellect that recognises only the testimony supplied by the senses and reasons from that alone'.[1] And probably the 'fog of our own creating' is but the dark veil of separateness arising from this blindness of the soul. The man who lacks reverence is blind, for if he

[1] J. Bruce Wallace in *Brotherhood*.

could see, he would have reverence; and the man who does not love is blind, for if he would see, he would love. In the Hall of Rest there came peace, and in the Hall of Silence there came understanding. These Halls are available to all here and now. If we can but enter the Hall of Rest, the senses are stilled, and we can then enter into the Silence, there to hear the 'still small voice', and to understand. 'Somewhere within the soul', we are told, 'there is silence. Attain unto it. It is a pearl of great price'. To enter into the Silence, to have vision, is necessarily to have reverence, to love, and to serve.

He urges us to control our affairs from without, to live widely, to pour ourselves away, not to live for self. 'The spiritual world is everywhere; the life of spirit is eternal, perfect, supreme.' 'The Christ spirit is everywhere, and yet, by some strange paradox, we are able to shut it out from our view.' 'We are unable,' says Private Dowding, 'to clear out our own poor thoughts and illusions and allow the Christ power to reflect through us'. And here the remark, 'You evidently know nothing about crystals. I cannot impress your mind with the wonders of this place,' is of far-reaching interest as indicating the need of the faculty to understand before the interior realisation of anything becomes possible.

In the presence of the 'powers of darkness' he finds it necessary to *empty himself of self*. 'Gain control of self,' he tells us, 'then retain control by emptying yourself of self.' On the Mount of Vision the Reservoirs of Illumination nearly blind him. He says: 'I feel I cannot, dare not, return. I cannot *unself* myself sufficiently.' In the first of these experiences, the self he speaks of, the self that is illusion, the sense-self, is *drawn* by the lure of the power of evil, and in the other it is *blinded* by the Light of the Reservoirs of Illumination. He returns to his 'own place alone, by the force of an interior gravity'. There is nothing indefinite, and there is much to ponder over in these experiences. We are told with the same certainty that vast spiritual purifying powers are waiting to be poured forth. 'Create vessels for this purpose', says Private Dowding. 'Make yourself a vessel that you may receive the gift of the spirit. . . . Retire into the Hall of Silence. Think on these things. Think on these things.' It is difficult to place too high a value on this teaching.

On page 36 he says, 'I ask you to mark the Messenger's words. He spoke of what he knew. Let his words blaze forth a channel through the minds of men. I ask this of you : to make them known.' What is it that he is so definitely anxious to make known? The message of the existence of Reservoirs of Light, of the uttering of the Word, or the illumination about to spread through East and West, or of the establishment of unity and universal peace? Perhaps all of these things. And whether the Reservoirs of Illumination be the latent but unawakened and therefore unexpressed spiritual strength and capacity of the races we cannot tell, but the uttering of the Word and the coming of the Revealer of the Word brings illumination nevertheless surely to the hearts of men.

It is true that great spiritual movements were initiated last century. One of the most remarkable of these has centred in the East round the Persian prophet Baha'u'llah. This Messenger of God has returned to his own high place, but his message of brotherhood and love begins to stir the hearts of men. Many of his prophecies have already been fulfilled. The ideals of unity and brotherhood for which he stood are spreading widely, despite the war. His Book of Laws remains to be made known to the world, but the inspiration which called it forth is certainly divine in origin. Baha'u'llah's son, the explainer of the message, whose name is Abdul Baha Abbas (servant of God), still dwells among men, controlling and directing the promulgation of a spiritual movement that seems likely to encircle the globe with the great ideal of unity. And in the West many movements of a spiritual and progressive order are now developing.

The Messenger tells us that the light dawns within individuals first, and that its radiance spreads, that outwardly its influence will show itself in many great reforms, and that 'great lamps will shine forth in East and West'. And again I would say in Private Dowding's words: 'Vast spiritual powers are waiting to be poured forth. Create vessels for this purpose. Make yourself a vessel that you may receive the gift of the spirit.' And I would close by repeating what he says with reference to love, which, in my opinion, seals the whole experience with the stamp of truth. 'If you would dwell in peace, learn to love deeply. Never cease loving. Love God by pouring yourself away. Love your fellows by giving them all you possess of light and truth. Love LOVE for her own blessed sake. Such love will bring you nearer heaven.'

W.T.P.

BOURNEMOUTH.
   19th March 1917.

PART III

The Messenger

20th March 1917, 8 p.m.

N O T long after Private Dowding's farewell visit, it began to dawn upon me that, as he could not return himself, he was trying to set up direct communication between the being whom he called the 'Messenger' and myself.

I have therefore held myself receptive in the hope of securing some further news of my friend, and I now set down the message that has reached me. I will reserve comment until later. * * *

Yes, I am the Messenger, and am speaking to you at your friend's special request.

W.T.P. May I ask a few questions?

Messenger. I am here to answer them.

W.T.P. Do you really see brighter times ahead for the human race?

Messenger. My son, you need have no fear. Your world is now plunged in grief and chaos. The hour is dark, the outlook strangely gloomy. We can see the light behind the thunder-clouds. Improvement in world-conditions is already taking place despite the war. Few kings will be left in Europe or, for that matter, anywhere. Russia will lead her people toward peace and emancipation. The illumination of a New Day will be reflected in the soul of the Slavonic race and will become apparent everywhere. In time to come

47

the dawn will break over Germany and the Northern peoples, sweeping before it the cruel darkness of ignorance and despotism.

Tribulation will be great; revolutions must be expected, but nothing can withstand the light. Vast changes lie ahead. Were I to tell you of these miracles, you would not credit them. We see regeneration in Persia, transformation in India; uprisings in the Far East and new discoveries; revolutionary events in the New World, North and South; but the light will grow.

France rises again purified, uplifted, and becomes the inspirer of the world in arts and sciences. Ireland comes into her own at last and becomes the cradle for great men and women. England joins hands with many nations in raising the standard of unity and fellowship among the peoples of the world. She will be called upon to make immense sacrifices, East and West, but she grows to a new greatness through her acts of renunciation.

Democratic republics will rule the world with free and peaceful intercourse between the nations. Peace does not yet come into her own, but the floodgates of God's love have been opened, and the divine power is for all nations.

Fear not the breaking down of barriers everywhere. Make the paths straight! The Lord of lords is destined to make a divine progress, and the ways must be prepared.

W.T.P. This is all very wonderful.

How will this new spiritual radiance make itself manifest?

Messenger. You are already witnessing its leavening power. The world is not in such darkness as it was even five years ago, and this despite the warring of the nations.

The light dawns within individuals first and then the radiance spreads. Outwardly its influence will show itself in many great reforms. In time the very air will become purer. Climates will improve; disasters caused by earthquakes, sea and air will slowly diminish; but there will be cataclysms first. Conflicts between religions will cease, the bitterness of sect will die away.

Women will hold equal rights with men. Great women, inspirers of the race, will rise up in East and West. Diseases—physical, mental, political, social—will gradually disappear. This must sound incredible to you. Remember that a spiritual remedy is becoming available for human sins and discords. It will veritably prove the elixir of the new age and will be within reach of all mankind. The Christ spirit will dwell among men with healing in its wings.

W.T.P. Why do you tell me all this?

Messenger. Eyes must be opened; ears must be attuned to the message of the coming day. Knowledge of the joy and peace that lie ahead will help you through these days of sore distress. By a consecrated act of faith bring understanding and wholeness into your own life and the lives of those around you.

W.T.P. Will the barriers between this world and the next be broken down?

Messenger. The veils are already thinning. As the race becomes regenerated from within, all need for barriers will disappear, and death will lose its awful sting.

The piercing of the veils should come about through spiritual and natural processes of mind and heart, and not through the employment of magic, ritual, or trance.

W.T.P. Will a new religion become necessary?

Messenger. The spirit will re-illuminate all religious faiths. The new religion will be one of service, fellowship, and unity.

W.T.P. And Egypt?

Messenger. The land of the Pharaohs has still a part to play in the evolution of the race, but it may not be through British influence. There are vast preparations now being made for the enlightened progress of the whole Moslem world.

W.T.P. How long will this take?

Messenger. I am not a very high being, and to me are not revealed details of all these wonderful happenings. So far as I am allowed to see, peace will be re-established during 1919.

Although actual fighting may end in 1918, it will take many years yet to bring poise and peace into actual and permanent being.

W.T.P. Who are you?

Messenger. I am one of those commanded to direct the new illumination into the avenues leading down towards the hearts and minds of men. I greet and protect certain souls, chosen for special work, as they reach this shore.

W.T.P. Was Thomas Dowding one of them?

Messenger. We met by what you would call 'accident'. He is making quick progress, and his power of service to his fellow-men will be great. It is often the most unexpected people who are chosen for important work.

W.T.P. What about the Far East?

Messenger. A great leader rises up in the time to come, and will avert many dangers. This one is long expected, and will bring about moral and social progress in China and elsewhere. The flames now visible between the Orient and the New World will ultimately be transmuted, purified, and harnessed to fine ends.

W.T.P. America?

Messenger. Her hour of tribulation is at hand. A splendid destiny will come into view. So long as material wealth remains the idol, so long will the light be held back. You must expect revolutions of a peculiar order at no distant date.

W.T.P. May we return to Germany?

Messenger. Already the world faintly perceives the probable progress of events in that land. Germany as an empire ceases to exist, but as a federation her future and ultimate well-being are assured. The days are still dark, but remember this: the greater the darkness of the night the greater the brilliance of the dawn.

W.T.P. And how are all these wonders to be brought about? Are we to expect prophets and teachers in our midst?

Messenger. Great lamps will shine forth in East and West. The period of revelations is upon you. The light is for the whole race, but individuals must reflect it within themselves, that it may become readily available for all.

Rise up and proclaim the dawn of the New Day! You can all become prophets and seers in this new dispensation. 'The people that walked in darkness have seen a great light; they that dwell in the land of the shadow of death, upon them hath the light shined.'

Physical birth and death are not for ever. Generation and dissolution as known to you will be transformed, transfigured. Herein dwelleth a mystery that cannot yet be unveiled. The road to its unveiling is the pathway of spotless purity.

W.T.P. Will your words be understood or believed?

Messenger. The wonders to be revealed are such that the peoples' vision will become unclouded and the sun's rays will shine through the minds and hearts of men and women. Then belief will become understanding.

W.T.P. What about social evils and injustices, poverty and ignorance, lust and greed? Can all these become transmuted?

Messenger. My son, have faith. Realise that the love of God is indeed all-powerful. The Golden Age will not be ushered in in the twinkling of an eye, as is thought by some. The law of evolution must be respected and cannot yet be overruled.

Extremes of wealth and poverty will disappear. Yes, this is so. The war itself has become a 'celestial instrument', as you have already been told. Governments will become simpler, less unwieldy, localised, filled with the ideals of justice and brotherhood.

The Oneness of Humanity, as emphasised by the great prophet who manifested last century, will become recognised, and as a result of this, vast reforms, social and ethical, will gradually be introduced throughout the world.

W.T.P. What about food?

Messenger. Grossness will disappear. The race will learn to live more simply on the blessed fruits and herbs and cereals. Unless the race learns this important lesson, it will be found that the earth cannot support the populations now inhabiting it. Over-eating and over-indulgence in the sense desires must cease.

The inspiration of the spiritual in life will take away the

need for the domination of the grosser appetites. Set the example! Fight the good fight! Increase your faith. To the God-endowed man all things are possible.

W.T.P. Your utterances are *so* utopian that I fear it impossible to secure a fair hearing for them.

Messenger. Compare 1817 with 1917. Compare 1900 with 2000 A.D. The latter comparison is only possible through the exercise of faith and vision. Much that I have foreshadowed will have become visible before the year 2000 A.D. My son, I give you my blessing and wish you God-speed.

N.B.—I have set down these very utopian sentiments and prophecies exactly as they flowed through my pen; but, although I am an optimist, I find it difficult to believe that the race is nearing the realisation of so many of its cherished ideals.

The prophecies are interesting despite their vagueness and extreme optimism. It is useless for me to do more than place them before my readers, and allow time to set its seal of truth or falsity upon them. Certainly we live in strange times, when all things are possible, when even the wildest dreams may be fulfilled before our eyes.

W.T.P.

BOURNEMOUTH.

20th March 1917.

PART IV

Private Dowding Returns

H.M.T. INDARRA, MEDITERRANEAN,
22nd May 1919, 10 a.m.

I AM allowed to return to you at last. Will you bear with me? There are many things I wish to say.

I am now enrolled among those who are attempting to pierce the curtain that separates your world from where we live. This work is being carried on from your side too. When I spoke to you before I had just arrived here. I was confused, bewildered. I was filled with shame and humiliation, my life on your side had been so useless.

The story of my passing across the barriers must have sounded confused, yet I am told that it has proved useful to many. I am glad if this is so. I have met a soldier recently arrived, who tells me he has read my book! He said it had been sent to him in Mesopotamia and was read eagerly by many of his pals. When he was dying of fever, feeling that his end was near (he now knows it was the beginning) he determined if life continued to search me out. And we have met!

I will not repeat this soldier's description of his arrival here. In some ways his experiences were similar to my own. I was glad I could help him. It was this soldier who persuaded me to try to speak to you again. His confidence in the value of the previous messages inspired me to search you out once more.

I asked the Messenger if I might try to find you. He told me to follow my own instincts—then I met your friend J.C. He said he was in touch with you. He brought me to your boat upon the Nile. We met again and you promised to listen for my message during your voyage from Egypt to England. I am here. J.C. promises to help to keep the channel open so that my thoughts may reach you clearly. He works with a group of officers among those emerging from the mists of your earth. I will take up my story from the time I left you. There may be those among your friends to whom the story of my life and training here may prove helpful. I was bitterly disappointed when I could no longer see or speak to you. The mists rose up between us. Now I see how well it was—I was befogged, not fit to speak to you, unlearned and unresigned. Do not be afraid of disappointments. The personal self puts in the sting without which disappointment would not cause depression. When disappointments descend upon you, look up, until your vision clears. Then you will understand and be at peace. The Messenger came for me. He told me he had spoken to you direct, that you had listened to his words. He said my message and his forecasts would be given to your world. I asked him to let me help break down the barriers. He took me to a hall of instruction that I had never seen before. The hall was crowded. Those present wished to learn how to return to the realm of mists between the worlds, to help new arrivals and to prepare the way for communion between souls already here and their friends on earth. It will be useful to tell you how we were trained to do this work. I give you my own experience, not because it has special value, but because it is my own. The Messenger led me to the centre of the hall. There the Teacher stood with pupils sitting around him, in ever widening circles, in eastern fashion.

The Teacher was dressed in a shining robe of flaming blue. When he spoke, orange and violet rays of light spread from him throughout the hall. He was an initiate. I hardly dared to look at him. I bowed my head. He took me by the hand. The Messenger told him of my desire. I was led to a seat in the fourteenth circle and sat down.

I cannot tell you all that happened and must leave much to your imagination. Do not be afraid of imagination. Correctly trained it proves a useful servant—I found myself sitting in a row of soldiers who had come over early in the war. They were all strangers to me. Two sitting near me have become my constant companions and we now work together in the mists.

I will tell you their stories later. I promised them I would. They have been profoundly interested in those first messages I sent you.

I will tell you what we learnt in the hall of instruction; how we were prepared for 'Active Service' on the 'battle-fields' between the worlds. . . .

The Teacher 'spoke' to us through signs and symbols, by pictures and by colour rays and by what seemed like etheric photographs upon a screen. Our training was divided into three parts. It has lasted a long time and is not yet over, although some among us have already taken up our work.

In the first lessons we were instructed how to discipline our own emotions and desires. This is very difficult. No worker is allowed to return into the mists for service until the emotions have been disciplined. We were instructed on the relation between the mind and the will. We were told how to empty ourselves until God's Mind and Will could be reflected through us without thought of self.

It was very difficult for me. It still is. Oh, my friend, I have much to learn—I have gone such a little way since we met last! I am glad to be allowed to speak to you again. Never mind if people tell you that 'Private Dowding' has no existence outside your own imagination. It does not matter. The message matters, fragmentary though it is. Give it and leave the rest. . . . The Teacher showed us his own mind. It was polished like crystal and reflected many pure rays of light from the celestial sphere. He showed us how to empty our minds of useless thoughts, poor ideals, and vain images. He showed us on a screen the mind of a man still living within the fleshly veil. (Screen is the wrong word: it was an oval crystal globe in which we saw the movements of chains of thoughts within the mind.)

This man represented a type. He was a successful merchant full of the desire to make more money, ambitious, without thought for the spiritual wider worlds around him. His mind revolved for us to study. Here is one trail of thoughts I followed:

'If peace is signed soon I will visit New York and open a branch there; that will come in useful when Jack comes into the business; lucky he was too young to fight, wish the school bills were not so heavy; shall cut out the University now; wish I had a second boy, too many girls; it can't be helped now, must try and get them married soon; what was that Ada (his wife) told me this morning about young Mr. Morgan? Wonder what his father's worth? I might find out, used to be on 'Change, but the war may have broken him; Johnson may know, Johnson hasn't paid that bill, must ring him up; wish I could afford a rest, this life is killing me and I cannot afford a partner or I'd take in George (his wife's brother), but then he's always been a rolling stone; suppose I must take him to the Club, I promised I would, but he plays rotten golf and is not too presentable; where did I leave my clubs? Must have been at Brighton, will telephone and find out, a man is given no peace and all those bills to meet on Saturday. Must see the bank again; so Warren's boy's been killed, hard lines; thank God my boy's safe at school. . . .'

That trail of thought went on a long way. This man's mental life was made up of almost endless chains of thoughts leading nowhere in particular. His mind was filled with unessentials. He had no time for thoughts beyond those which revolved continually around himself, his worldly interests, and his people. His was not a vicious mind, simply uncontrolled, self-centred, unillumined. It was shown to us as a common type. The Teacher then showed us a similar mind belonging to a man who had just come across. He was lost in the mists. Some of the senior students among us went out into the mists to help him. He was a wanderer, without home or peace. It was long before the chains could be broken and the man released from the meshes of his mind. Now he is a student here, filled with the desire to make his life of service to his fellow-men. By this and similar examples, showing the working of the human mind, we were instructed. Human will-power and its relation to the emotions; the cleansing of the human mind from sensuality; how to reflect within ourselves God's Will, and through *that* Will (and not our own) to harness and purify the emotional life—all this we learnt gradually. Sometime you shall hear more. It is full of interest. I will return each day while the voyage lasts.

23rd *May* 1919, 11 a.m.

Before telling you about the second and third part of our training I should like to talk to you on other matters. About yourself: you have come through the war not unscathed but safe. How wonderfully you have been protected. At one time I expected you over here, but it was a mistake. Then I asked to be allowed to speak with you again. So the war is over! Is it really over? Here it looks as if the struggle were still continuing: not perhaps on outer battlefields but in men's hearts and minds. This struggle will go on for a long time. What absorbs my thoughts is the wonderful development of interest in what you call the unseen now going on in English-speaking lands on earth. We hope to pierce the veils, to break down useless barriers, but this work needs careful training. I will speak more of this. Balanced minds are so essential. How rarely found! But who am I to speak? I know so little and am still a child! Many warnings have been given us as to the methods of our work. Some of these warnings I shall pass over to you. Make them known or the good work will be delayed. These warnings may be voiced by me through you, but they come from my Teacher and the Messenger.

The Messenger has become my guide; am I not fortunate? He comes to me at times when I am resting.

My life is now divided into three parts: one spent in the hall of instruction, another in the land of the mists helping to dispel the fog and tumult, and the third in the gardens of rest, where I have a little house and garden of my own. We construct our own surroundings here by the creative power of our own thoughts. You are doing the same although it is not so apparent to you. I repeat: you construct your own surroundings even in that opaque and circumscribed outer world by your own thinking. Where do your chains of thoughts lead? Are they chains holding you down or are they threads of light leading you upward? I still find myself involved in my own chains—the after effect of my useless life on earth. Take warning from my experiences. When I come again I will tell you more about the School.

23rd May 1919, 9 p.m.

I will not give you an account of the instruction given to us by our Teacher. I cannot remember it all. Some of the thoughts left in my mind as the result of time spent in the hall of instruction will leave their trace upon you and through you upon others who may read what you set down. Many of the lessons in selflessness, self-control, the relation between reason and intuition, between intellect and emotion, are lessons which we should have learnt while still on earth. I spoke to you before about the supreme importance of emptying oneself of self in order to reflect the Divine Mind—and this lesson was drilled into us by the Teacher as of immense importance. Only those of us who had achieved some measure of understanding were allowed to leave the hall of instruction and spend some time as novices among the workers in the intermediary realm. The Teacher often accompanied us on these occasions. He showed how to protect ourselves from turbulent sensual and fearful thoughts which shot in and out among the mists like crimson darts. Until we could protect ourselves from such attacks we were unable to protect others.

The darkness caused by fear and hate and lust forms itself into pungent gases (I must use your terms) so that we often nearly lost consciousness. It is difficult to protect oneself against these dense vibratory conditions brought over into the mist realm by human souls in torment. The torments suffered by so many result from ignorance, from fear of the passage from one world to the next, also from what I call soullessness. This latter condition is only apparent and does not last for ever. It is seen among those who have lived utterly selfish or evil lives on your earth. I do not wish to dwell upon such conditions. They are met over here by purgatorial tests which gradually purify and ultimately release the souls in torment. Purgatory, unlike Hell, is a condition to be welcomed, to be bravely faced and lived through. I am beginning to rise above my own purgatory; otherwise I could be of no real service to others.

The second part of our training was carried on in the mists which hang over the great River separating your world from ours. All souls must pass through these mists on leaving their physical form for the last time. Three times I have succumbed to the influence of that dark sphere; my light has become shrouded and my mind darkened. On each occasion two of my fellow-workers carried me into a hall of healing where I slowly recovered consciousness and was able to return to my own home. Had I been selfless the evil conditions could not have overcome me. We must train ourselves so that fear and sensual thoughts will find no response within our minds and fall annihilated by their own inherent lifelessness. Remember that all evil thoughts and forms have no life of their own. They disappear so soon as this truth is recognised and applied. The task of workers in the mists is to destroy the (apparent) power of conditions created by discordant human thinking; to light up the avenues leading from one world to the next with the torches of love, truth, and wisdom. These Avenues need not be full of sorrow, fear, and darkness. They must become illumined by the true joy of life and understanding so that the sting of death shall disappear. I have more to tell you about this region. Many still in the flesh are called upon to work there with us during both waking and sleeping hours. I want to impress upon you the importance of such work. Next time I will speak of the third portion of our training.

24th May 1919, 9 p.m.

Beyond the hall of instruction a great avenue of trees leads up a mountain-side. Upon the hill is set a mansion known to us as our temple of initiation. When the group or circle to which I belong had been tested in the mists and had been taken through the under world (where further tests awaited us), the Teacher called us together in the hall of instruction, and we were each given a new robe to wear, a sign that we were on the path toward the first gateway of initiation. This language is symbolic. A thread of actual events runs through the symbolism. I wonder whether this has any value for you? I fear to be misunderstood. The conditions of life here cannot be explained in terms of time, space, or form, as you know these. Set down what I tell you; pass it on if you feel able. Despite much that will seem confused, here and there may be found a helpful thought. There is much cause for hope! Ever since I spoke through to you two years ago (according to your measurements of time) the veils between us have thinned and many on both sides are now engaged upon this splendid work.

The Teacher arrayed us in our new and living robes and spoke of what lay ahead. We prayed together for illumination and the power to make our lives of greater service. It was a solemn happy moment. We passed out into the avenue that stretched between the hall of instruction and the temple of initiation.

I must not dwell upon the various tests put to each one of us before we were allowed within the temple. Nor can I tell you much that happened there. These experiences will come to many of you.

There were nine of us in the group, all that had passed the tests, out of eighty-one in the fourteenth circle in the hall of instruction. We were welded into an instrument of succour—we were initiated into spiritual mysteries—we were shown a portion of the plan, a small fragment of which we are destined to fulfil. Each one of the nine was allotted a special task and place in the ranks of the army of liberation. Our task is to free souls from the chains of their selfish thoughts which hang around them miserably upon their arrival on the borderland. You and many like you are members of this glorious army.

In the hall of initiation our teacher handed us over to a Master who opened the doorways of our inner understanding. Of this I can tell you nothing now. Remember how sad and broken I was when I first came over here! Now I have my use and can share my joy with you. Take heart, all who still find themselves enshrouded in the gloomy canopies of self!

At the Master's bidding an angel showed us the conditions surrounding the various states of Illumination, the variations of light and colour that could most effectively destroy the various kinds of darkness.

We were shown how to protect our own minds from gloom and fear; how to *reflect* light through our every thought and deed. We were instructed how to meet and transmute the evil gases let loose in the purgatorial regions by thoughts of fear and sensuality. We were taken up into the temple tower and shown a vision of the glories of the seven celestial spheres.

I am only allowed to indicate vaguely what it means to pass through the first gateway of initiation on the path of selfless service. Is it not wonderful that I am here? Am I not fortunate to have been chosen for such glorious work? Do not wait until you come over. Start at once upon the pathway that will lead you to the temple of initiation. All true worlds are one and interpenetrate. . . . The Messenger is with me now. He says I must not speak further of this temple and its Master and the angels who help forward our interior illumination. Next time I will take you to my own home. We will talk of simple homely matters. Good night.

24th May 1919, 10 p.m.

Greeting! Come home with me. When I spoke through to you two years ago I had no settled home. I was a lonely wanderer, almost friendless and very sad. You helped me then. I often think of that with gratitude. Some day you must let me help you. I have been told something of the group to which you belong. You are doing useful work. [Private Dowding took me by the hand and led me along one of the main thoroughfares of the country region to which he belonged. I was quite conscious of my external surroundings sitting writing on the deck of a great liner on a stormy sunny sea, but I was also conscious of that inner journey in thought regions in company with my friend who still prefers to be known as Private Dowding. Let the scoffer scoff. The time is coming when such experiences as these will be freely shared by many men and women, while still on earth. I am not afraid to speak of them as part of my normal and natural life.—W.T.P.]

I love my little home. The Messenger helped me to create it. This path leads to it. Are not these mossy banks green and restful? A brook runs down one side. I have made friends with many of the water-fairies in the spring up on the mountain-side. Here is my little wood. I found it here when I first came. It was created by a radiant soul who has now passed joyfully to a higher sphere. The Messenger told me I could call it mine. It was a time when the words 'mine' and 'thine' still held a meaning for me!

Here above the wood on the hillside I have built my home. I want you to come in with me. That is my dog, my one faithful companion upon your earth. Have I never told you about him? He died while I was in France. I found him by accident soon after I came here. He recognised me and followed me. From that time all real loneliness has left me. I do not know if animals have immortal souls. I have much to learn. I can but relate my own experiences, and there is 'Frisker' full of life and spirits. [Frisker was a Manchester terrier who certainly seemed as alive as any dog could be, full of spirits and intelligence. W.T.P.] . . . Come into my home so that you can tell your friends about it! . . .

[Private Dowding led me through a garden filled with trees and flowers into a small bungalow.—(I must use these terms although they are quite inadequate and are only symbolical.) Steps led up into a wide porch through which we passed into a circular hall with a fountain in its centre.

There were flowers and pictures everywhere and deep com-
fortable seats in alcoves. A crystal globe stood upon a
pedestal in a great hearth. What seemed like fire or some
form of illumination played through the crystal globe from
the hearth behind, filling the house with radiance. There
were only four rooms in the bungalow, two on either side
of the hall. The first we entered was filled with books. Between the bookcases on the walls were mirrors—strange
mirrors about which I will speak later. It is in this room
that Dowding works and studies. The next room is where
he rests and dreams and renews his strength. The bow win-
dow gave upon a wonderful view stretching across the garden down the hillside over the tree-tops to a sapphire lake
in the green valley below.

I did not go into the two rooms on the left of the hall,
but Dowding told me they were guest chambers often used
by his two soldier pals who are now working in his group
of nine. He has already promised to introduce me to them
so that I may hear their stories.—W.T.P.]

I am so pleased you like my home. Come and sit in the
hall. That crystal has only been given to me recently. It
reflects many of the events going on around me in this
part of the country. The mirrors in my study reflect in
symbolic form the effects of great events and movements
taking place in your world. One recent event in London
has produced profound effects here. I have been looking at
some of them; first, the effect in your world in the mirrors
in my study, and then the resultant effects here, in the
crystal globe you are now looking at. I refer to the Albert
Hall Meeting held by Spiritualists to demonstrate the nearness of our world to yours and your world to ours and to

act as a memorial for the soldiers killed in battle. I was in the hall with my own group. We were among many similar groups. Thousands of disembodied soldiers were present. We were greatly moved.

The Messenger returned home with me when the meeting was over and gave me interesting advice and guidance. I will tell you some of the things he said next time we meet. . . .

25th May 1919, 10 a.m.

It appears that there are two methods by which you can lift the curtain and communicate with our world. The first is the one more commonly in use at present. I am repeating the Messenger's words, they are not my own. It is the automatic method, *i.e.* the use of trance mediums, certain mechanical devices, and automatic writing. The second method consists in the development of normal clairvoyance. This is safer. It leads to the best results. You are using what the Messenger calls the normal clairvoyant method in talking to me now.

The Messenger dwelt upon the dangers connected with automatic communication and the possibilities of fraud. The veil should be lifted by natural methods, by trained clairvoyant vision and clairaudience. It can also be safely lifted during sleep. Public sittings organised professionally with entrance fees should be discouraged. Remember the Messenger's words when with you last: 'The piercing of the veils should come about through spiritual and natural processes of mind and heart, and not through the employment of magic ritual or trance.'

There is usually one member of a family with deeper vision than the rest. There should be family groups everywhere. They should sit together in prayer and silence for half an hour on each Sunday or holy day, creating conditions that will enable us to approach. If one member of the family group passes over here, the other members should await his or her return, sitting together quietly in the usual way. When the time is ripe, communion will be established safely. . . .

There are dangers in the present situation. Thousands of untrained eager souls both here and with you are tearing at the veil. They use any methods that suggest themselves. Their thoughts and actions are uncontrolled. Desire outruns reason. Emotion upsets the will. 'Fools step in where angels fear to tread.' The Messenger feels strongly about this. I have been carefully trained before I could be employed on useful work. Schools of instruction are needed on your side too. Beware of a reaction from the present impetuous wave of interest in communication between the worlds. Telepathy between members of a family on earth should be practised. If A in London is able to speak to B in Sydney and B of Sydney passes over here, then direct communication can be set up very quickly. B remains asleep awhile, then awakes and thinks of A in London. If A has not forgotten B, he will 'hear' B's call, and conscious communication will be re-established. That is the natural way. It can be practised without danger of pulling B back into earth conditions. Contacts brought about through mediums are liable in time to delay the disembodied soul and to hold him near the earth atmosphere. I am speaking to you now from my own home which you have visited and described. I am sitting in my study impressing my thoughts upon your mind. You are visible to me on the mirror on my wall. I see you sitting at a table on a ship's deck. You are writing in a notebook. I can watch you clearly yet I am not earthbound nor am I dwelling in the land of mist. I am at home. You are where you are. We communicate by a natural method, by telepathy. It is well.

25th May 1919, 9 p.m.

The Messenger tells me that some of his forecasts are being fulfilled. I asked him to send you more to include with the messages I am sending you. He does not think it necessary.

People on earth, he says, already live too largely either in the past or in the future. Prophetic utterances are interesting, sometimes serviceable, often dangerous. Man must live the day and do his best uninfluenced by sad memories of the past or fearful thoughts about the future.

It is not easy. The present is the only real there is. If you but knew, both past and future are contained within it. I asked the Messenger for advice on healing work as you suggested. He says the time has not yet come for him to speak of this. I am becoming interested in spiritual healing work.

Now I will tell you the stories of my two friends, as promised. They do not wish their names disclosed. I will call them Captain Y and Sergeant Z (these ranks they held while fighting before coming here).

Captain Y shall tell his own story:

[I was conscious of another figure sitting with Dowding in his study—a tall man, wearing a similar cloak and robe to Dowding's and the same group star symbol on his breast—W.T.P.]

'I was a regular soldier and went out to France in 1914,

among the first. I was "killed" before the year was out. I
cannot tell you much about it. It was at night; we were re-
treating, my horse had been shot beneath me. I was standing looking down upon him when a shell exploded near me.
Nothing seemed to happen. I was still looking at my horse;
but he was alive again, which struck me as very strange.
I took him by the bridle, mounted and rode away. The
whole action was mechanical. I cannot give you many details. I was joined by another man I knew, also riding (a
brother officer who had been stunned by the same shell
and his horse killed, I discovered later). He asked me where
we were. I could not tell him. We soon knew that something
must have happened, but we did not think that 'death' had
overtaken us. We both thought we had lost our way in the
retreat and were wandering in strange country, dazed by
fatigue and lack of food. We had had no proper sleep or
food for four days. I was too dazed to wonder what would
happen next. Soon I fell asleep. I could not keep awake,
although I feared to sleep lest I should fall off my horse.
I awoke to find myself in what I now know to be a hall
of rest. My horse had disappeared, my companion also. It
was only recently that I heard he had not been killed at all,
but rendered unconscious by the shell that killed me. While
senseless he was able to be with me, riding on his own horse
that had been killed. He was taken prisoner but is now
released and well. I am trying to get through to him. There
is little more to tell you. I rested until my own guide found
me. He brought me to the hall of instruction where I have
spent much time. I learned slowly, it was all strange to me.
Then Dowding joined our circle and he has brought me
to you. We work together. Dowding will tell you about it.
There is no moral to my story. I came here quite simply,

without distress. I was sorry to leave your world, but I have many friends here and can work usefully. I have no more regrets and shall hope to be of service in the border-land where thousands remain in ignorance and misery.

'Conditions are improving and I am told the chaos in your world is to be stilled. We will do our best from here.'

Private Dowding. My sergeant friend is not here at present but I will tell you about him. He was drowned when the transport he was travelling in was mined. He says he made a big struggle to reach a raft but was unsuccessful.

He does not remember any feeling of distress whilst drowning, when once he had given up the struggle. He told me the actual sinking into unconsciousness was not unpleasant. Sergeant Z does not know how long he remained unconscious; he says his passing over was gentle, that he travelled through the land of mist without mishap whilst still in a dazed condition. It seems that his brother found him quickly and brought him through. A bond of great affection linked these two; a year separated their coming over. A bond of love between two souls, if it be unselfish, will achieve much. Through it the passing-out experience can be robbed of danger, made pleasant instead of fearful. Had I been met when I arrived my troubles would have been less severe. I *was* met, but I was too self-centred to pierce the fog of my own selfish thoughts which shut me in on all sides.

Sergeant Z now works with us. You can watch our group at work on the borderland where most of our time is spent. Keep in touch with us and when one in whom you are interested passes across we will be there to make the pathway easy. I will return later. . . .

26th May 1919, 10 a.m.

I would like to speak on spiritual healing. I am beginning to study this subject. I believe it will ultimately super-
sede drugs and surgery in your world. Here all healing
work is accomplished through allowing the mind to reflect
healing rays of light from higher spheres. It could be the
same in your world.

The Messenger tells me this is a subject in which you
are greatly interested. I hope you will give me your ideas.
I firmly believe that the healing of physical infirmities by
spiritual methods and the unbarring of the gateways between our world and yours will do more than all else to
bring about the speedy progress and happiness of the Race.
Do all in your power to bring this about!

The Messenger is with me now. Have you any question
you would like to ask him?

W.T.P. Do you wish these further messages from P.D.
published?

Messenger. It is our wish that every possible step should
now be taken to arouse interest among you in the realms
in which we dwell.

Mankind has concentrated thought too long upon what
can be felt and seen and heard in the material world to the
exclusion of all other interests. Life on earth can but last
a few score years at most. Men must prepare and train
themselves for the wider life whilst still on earth. Call attention to the conditions on this side of the veil so that
men may come over to their homes and not into a country
that is strange.

The thoughts and experiences of my son, known to you

as Private Dowding, should prove useful to many among you.

W.T.P. Was this why he was allowed to speak to me again?

Messenger. It is no longer a question of 'allowing'. Private Dowding has a settled abode among us and is doing good work. When he first arrived here he was not in a fit condition to communicate with your world because he had no understanding of his surroundings.

W.T.P. How do you view the present campaign among Spiritualists to break through the veil hiding your world from ours?

Messenger. It is a natural outcome of the war. As the Race grows in spiritual understanding the need for the veil will disappear. It is part of the Divine Plan that this should be so. * * * Breaks off here.

Private Dowding. I see that the conditions around you make it difficult for the Messenger's thoughts to reach your mind. (I was in the smoking-room which was crowded and noisy.) He will speak to you tonight when your body sleeps, and you can translate his thoughts into your language when conditions around you are more tranquil.

I have just returned home from the land of mist. I find work there most interesting. I left a man who was very anxious to return to your earth. He was killed in a street accident and is totally unprepared for his new life here.

Break again. . . . Conditions impossible.

P.D. promises to return tomorrow. . . .

27th *May* 1919, 10 a.m.

I am sitting in my study resting after a period of strenuous work in the borderland. It is important that this sphere should cease to be a land of mist and gloom. When the radiance from the realms above has become diffused throughout the borderland, a great task will have been achieved. Think what it will mean! I can tell you best by illustration. You have seen London enshrouded in thick yellow fog. Imagine this fog lasting day in, day out, so that all activities of life become subservient to it. Would not the whole life of the city become changed, impoverished? Imagine that at long last the fog lifted and brilliant sunshine bathed London night and day, without intervals of fog or rain or darkness. Would not the city and its inhabitants become transformed? When the thick mist lifts from the borderland between your world and ours, a new and more spiritual era will begin. The soul arriving will bathe in light and gravitate immediately to his own haven of rest and harmony. The fear of death will disappear. Man will pass across the river joyful and unafraid. Those he leaves behind him will watch his journey with eyes undimmed by tears. They will see the friends waiting to welcome him into the wider world. He will be allowed to relate his new and wonderful experiences to those he has left behind. There will be no fog between. Materialistic thinking and the fear of death have raised the barriers separating our life here from yours. All this must go. The fog has begun to lift! Help us to spread the radiance that will lift it altogether. The task is not impossible. Your world needs inspiration from higher realms. Often our best endeavours to pierce the veils and illumine dark places in the minds of men have borne no fruits. The fog has shut out the light and men on earth have lived in darkness or at least in twilight. This is, of course, symbolic. When the borderland becomes freed from gloom, filled with illumination, then a new era will begin on earth. Wars will cease. Disease and hatred will abate. Physical climates will improve. Discords of every kind will be replaced by harmony and progress. Men's vision will extend so that selfishness and greed will no longer seem attractive. Cannot you see what an important work this is: the thinning of the veils and the lighting of the borderland? The new era is upon us. The forces of evil are far spent. Light begins to pierce the gloom with which the minds of men have been filled so long. These are not empty words. The task before us remains stupendous, but the word has gone forth and we must obey our guides and masters. The powers of evil on your side and ours have fought to withstand the Light. At one time it seemed as if they would succeed. That danger is over now. The clouds that hid the sun will disappear in rain. This rain will purify the borderland, wash away impurity, and flow into the minds of men as new rivers of life and truth. The Messenger bids me tell you this. He speaks of what he knows. Make his words understood!

The Messenger is here and will speak to you.

W.T.P. Reference has been made to the formation of schools of instruction in our own world for training men and women to help bring about the spiritual transformation to which Dowding has just referred. How are these to come into existence?

Messenger. Every group of earnest students banded together on your side can attract to itself a guide from our spheres who will train and instruct them during waking hours and whilst the body sleeps. Each group should ask for unseen guidance and instruction. This will be given in various ways. It may come through books or friends at first. Soon a guide will gravitate to the group and make communication possible. When this has been brought about, the road will become easier. The guide will illumine the pathway to be trod by each member of the group. New groups will be formed, with each member of the older groups as a centre. Gradually the world will become encircled in this way. Each group will find itself in touch with a group of students already trained on our side of the veil. Purify and illumine your own thinking so that the mists may be cleared away. This work is directed and blessed by beings from the highest spheres. Once having set your hand to the plough do not turn back.

W.T.P. Will this work be carried on by the religious organisations of our world?

Messenger. This new campaign will be carried forward within existing organisations and without. Its progress will not be dependent on creeds or dogmas. It will shake itself free from superstition and bigotry. Your task is to carry on your own work without let or hindrance from other groups.

As time goes on the groups of workers on your side and ours will be linked harmoniously. The Light will spring from mind to mind. Nothing can withstand the coming illumination. [At this point the Messenger withdrew—.]

Note by W.T.P.

28th May 1919, 10 a.m.

The return of Private Dowding was not altogether un-expected by me. I had been conscious for some time past that he wished to communicate again. When he first spoke to me in March 1916 I found no difficulty in setting down what he wished to say. He seemed to stand beside me while I wrote his story down. On the present occasion the task has been more difficult. It is as if I had to catch Dowding's ideas as they fell from a great height. It is not always easy to translate the ideas into intelligible words.

Personally I am satisfied that it is Dowding who is com-municating with me again, but I can offer no proof of this statement. I set down this record for what it may be worth but claim nothing for it. I have been in the habit of sitting in silence in the 'quiet room' on my Nile boat each Sunday. On these occasions many friends from the wider world have visited me and my companion F.L.

On the first Sunday in June 1919 a regular visitor, J.C., spoke to me about Dowding and said he would bring him to the boat. On a subsequent occasion Dowding came. He was no longer dressed in a private's uniform but in a blue cloak with flowing robe beneath and the star emblem of his group upon his breast. Dowding seemed delighted to find that he could speak through to me again. He promised to tell me about his present life, and when I told him I was going home by long sea route he promised to visit me daily during the voyage. This promise has been carried out, and although the ship is so overcrowded that conditions are not good, yet I hope I have been able to clothe Dowding's thoughts in words that can be understood.

I do not know that there is anything very new or striking about the present series of messages received from Private Dowding. They are interesting in that they show how his outlook has widened since he first arrived in a new world. I also think that his remarks about the borderland are useful and may help to clear up misconceptions about that strange place. Dowding's outlook on life has grown more optimistic and the Messenger still seems satisfied that the Race is approaching a new and golden era. All my experiences in the intermediary realm that separates (whereas it should join) our world from the wider world, lead me to the conclusion that Dowding is correct in what he says on page 62 about materialistic thinking and the fear of death.

There is one other subject I should like to comment upon. On page 68 the Messenger dwells upon the dangers connected with automatic communication between the worlds. He strongly urges the need for the development of what is called normal clairvoyance and clairaudience if the best results are to be obtained.

I have had some experience of both the automatic and the natural methods to which both he and Dowding refer and can thoroughly endorse all that is said in this connection.

The greater my experience of group work (referred to on page 77 and elsewhere) the surer I am that this is by far the sanest and safest method for piercing the veils and for developing natural clairvoyance.

May I be allowed to repeat the warning given in the first part of Private Dowding's messages as to the time factor?

That a new era is dawning upon this sad and storm-tossed world is now apparent. The dawn will still be dawn and not full daylight for many years to come. References made to the swift progress of the Race must not be interpreted too literally. The time factor cannot be gauged with any degree of accuracy even by the denizens of the wider worlds. Finally, may I be allowed on Private Dowding's behalf to thank all those people who have written to express their appreciation of the messages that he has given to the World. I hope that the present message will receive as friendly a reception as the previous one.   W.T.P.

PART V

The Passing of Major P.

T O the January and April numbers of *The Quest* (1915), Mr. E. E. Fournier d'Albe contributed two illuminating articles on the 'Negative Evidence for Survival' of life after the dissolution of the physical body. He sums up his case by saying that 'Death is the cessation, not of life, but of our communication with it'.

Now the question arises as to whether there is any necessity for this communication to cease? If we take it for granted that there is no negative evidence against the possibility of survival, is it possible to discover any positive evidence for survival?

At the outset of any attempt to investigate the conditions of life immediately following physical death, the student is faced with almost overwhelming difficulties. What would appear to be first-hand and positive evidence to the investigator himself becomes of necessity second-hand and therefore almost valueless to those who attempt to follow his researches. In other words, the individual can prove the continuation of life beyond physical dissolution only by his own personal experience; the experiences related by his fellows cannot be considered by him as either final or conclusive. This fact raises a barrier that cannot easily be broken down, and greatly complicates all research work into the regions that lie just on the other side of physical death.

After all, the crucial question is: Can you or I actually

obtain first-hand evidence of such survival? For who can watch beside a death-bed or on the battlefield, the passing-away of life from the body, without speculating on the after-death conditions of that life?

The province of the present writer, however, is not to construct a theoretical thesis or to enter into an argument in favour of survival or otherwise, but rather to give an account, in language as simple as possible, of certain experiences that recently fell to his lot. The scientific explanation of the phenomena to be described pertains to a future generation; at present no one can presume to dogmatise. But surely the time has come for attempting in some measure to grapple in a positive and reasonable manner with this great problem!

The writer was recently brought into close touch with the case of an officer who in the prime of life was struck down by a fatal disease, and the following description of his 'passing-over' is taken from notes made by the writer at the time. He felt in close touch with the dying man for several weeks both preceding and following the actual passing-away.

The writer cannot attempt to explain how or why the following experiences came to him. Whether they were telepathic or otherwise, it is impossible for him to say. They are simply set down in the exact order in which they were 'seen' or 'heard'.

Before going further, it should be stated that the editor of *The Quest* has in his possession full details of the case— Major P.'s name, the address of the house in which he died, and so far as is practicable has satisfied himself as to the *bona fides* of these experiences.

If the notes that follow are not an actual first-hand account of the passing-away of life from the physical body, what are they? Hallucination? Yes, possibly, but after all that is simply a label and not an explanation in itself. In any case, the writer has set down exactly what he believes actually did take place, both just before and just after the physical dissolution of Major P., and readers are left to form their own conclusions. The notes naturally fall into two divisions:

1. A descriptive account of the phenomena, observed by the present writer, during Major P.'s passing-away.

2. Experiences purporting to be those of the dying man himself, and, so far as was possible to ascertain them, what seemed to be his sensations after he had actually passed out of his physical body.

I

Major P. had been ill for several months, but was in full possession of his faculties until a few days before death, when repeated injections of morphia produced a state of coma. The following account is set down from the writer's rough notes, which as stated above, were made at the time— that is, *within a few hours of the actual events themselves.*

22*nd March*, 3 *p.m.*   Death seems very close at hand, and there is no apparent sign of consciousness. Directly above the dying man I can see a shadowy form that hovers in a horizontal position about two feet above the bed. This form is attached to the physical body on the bed by two transparent elastic cords. One of them appears to be attached to the solar plexus and the other to the brain. As I watch this form it grows more distinct in outline, until I can see that it is an exact counterpart, so far as form is concerned, of the body on the bed. I can see what look like spiral currents passing up through these two cords, and as the physical body grows more lifeless, the form hovering above seems to become vital.

3.15 *p.m.* Two figures have now appeared, and stand one on either side of the bed against the wall. They are tall and radiant, but these forms seem to my vision to be of some finer form of 'matter' than the 'double' that is hovering above the bed.

3.40 *p.m.* This 'double' has become still more distinct; I can see that the 'cords' are still attached to Major P.'s body, and the currents referred to above have now gathered considerable upward momentum. The life-force is steadily ebbing out of the body, and is apparently passing into the form above.

3.55 *p.m.* The two figures stoop down over the bed and seem to break off the 'cords' at points close to the physical body. Immediately I see that the form or double rises about two feet from its original position, but remains horizontal, and at this same moment Major P.'s heart stops beating.[1]

So far as I can see, Major P.'s 'life-currents' have been drawn out from his body, and have passed up through the two luminous cords into the 'double' or subtle body that has just been described. This form is still hovering above the bed, but the life within it shows no sign of outward consciousness.

4.30 *p.m.* I can no longer see the two figures that were present both before and at the moment of death, but what I take to be the 'soul' of the dead man seems to be asleep within its new garment, and is totally dissociated from the body on the bed.

---

[1] For several hours before this, there had been no apparent consciousness or outward sign of life.

10.30 *p.m.*   Dissolution of the material body has already begun. I can still see the 'new' body in the death-chamber, but it is no longer quite so distinct in outline. It appears to be asleep.[1]

No further notes were recorded until about 10 a.m. on 23rd March.

23*rd March,* 10 *a.m.*   There seems to be some disturbance in the conditions around Major P., but he does not wake to a realisation of his new state of 'consciousness'.

12 *midday.*   The sleeping form is drawn back toward earth-conditions, and becomes more 'opaque' in appearance. A sort of 'fluctuation', an ebb and flow, is going on, but I cannot explain in detail what I mean by these terms as applied to a purely non-physical phenomenon.

4 *p.m.*   I can see two great luminous 'wings' outstretched over Major P.'s sleeping form, and they appear to be providing protection against some possible danger.

7 *p.m.*   I can no longer see Major P., either in the death-chamber or out of it, but I am quite conscious of his 'existence', and am fully aware, in some remarkable manner, of the conditions by which he now appears to be surrounded. For instance, I am fully convinced that the form in which he now finds himself has become more luminous (while it still resembles in outline the physical body he has just left); but I cannot prove to myself, or to anyone else, from what source this conviction has reached me.

24*th March,* 8 *a.m.*   Major P. seems to be drawn back until he again appears as actually present in the house and

[1] For the sake of convenience, from this point onwards, the term Major P. is to be taken as referring, not to the dead body, but to the life within what might be called the 'ethereal' body that has just been described.

in the death-chamber itself. His form is still 'lying' in an apparently reclining posture.

4 *p.m.* The 'wings' are still there, full of light and colour—rose and violet, clear orange and royal blue; they seem to prevent the approach of evil influences and also to act as a protection against the loving but inevitably mistaken desire of those left behind that he should return to them.

7 *p.m.* Another figure is watching and waiting near Major P., who is not yet fully awake. It seems to be that of a friend who died some time ago. He will, I feel, be useful in explaining the new conditions of life to the new arrival.

It is curious that I cannot communicate with this figure.

25th March, 2.30 *a.m.* There are signs of waking. The 'guardians' (the two 'figures') return; there is movement of the form and probably there will soon be semi-consciousness. I am fully aware of all this, although, physically speaking, I can no longer 'see' anything.

6.30 *a.m.* Movement and impulsive semi-unconscious response to 'thought-waves' from this side. Prayer and protection though are invaluable at such a time.

10 *a.m.* A state of quiescent semi-consciousness. No memory of illness or death, but a hazy sensation of lying asleep in bed at home. There is no curiosity, very little memory, only rest and peace, and a curiously subtle feeling of *security*.

12 *midday*. Slight memory returns, and with it a vision of home. A slight feeling of distress, probably due to the great grief and suffering of some loved one. Now for the first time curiosity and speculation begin to assert themselves, but more sleep follows. An awakening to fuller con-

sciousness seems imminent, and the breathlessness of first impressions is in the air.

3 *p.m.* More complete consciousness, and an anxiety to use and to understand new powers and possibilities.

For the first time conscious volition and movement are noted. Then a sudden wave of memory relating to earth-life matters, and as suddenly as a flash the wave is gone, leaving no apparent trace. Whilst it lasted it was possible for the writer to arrest certain impressions that related to those on earth. They took the form of messages to his own family, and being of a private and personal nature are not inserted here.

4 *p.m.* More sleep follows, but Major P. is getting accustomed to his new 'garment' and surroundings, and although all memory of the past is wiped out, temporarily at least, yet perhaps it is more merciful so, because otherwise the memories of earth-life might draw the soul back to earth-conditions, making progress and development difficult. Probably memory will return, but in a more subtle and less crude form, and he may be unconsciously (or otherwise) allowed to help his people in their great grief and loneliness. But it is unlikely, and not very wise, that there should be any definite or direct messages, nor should these be asked for, because nothing can be gained on either side by drawing the soul back to earth-conditions.

7 *p.m.* The 'guardians' are still there. Also the other watcher, referred to above, is trying gradually to obtain response and recognition. It is becoming difficult to 'sense' the conditions around the newly awakened soul, and still more difficult to describe them adequately in an intelligible manner.

There seems to be no memory of the earth-life, nor of

the body left behind, and the soul, whose passing-over we have been trying to describe, has no knowledge of his own body's funeral, nor of earth-conditions generally.

The foregoing notes will probably appear more intelligible when considered in relation to the experience that is given under the second heading.

As explained earlier, the following account is based upon the dying man's own experiences and sensations so far as it was possible to gather them, and is given exactly as 'received'.

The account is chaotic, vague, and somewhat hysterical, but is this to be wondered at in the circumstances? Who could give a careful analysis and controlled description of such, for them, stupendous happenings?

⁂

I I

'I have been laid up a long time, and am becoming indifferent to matters of material moment that used to be of such absorbing interest to me. The pain of illness is at times acute, and on the whole I rather look forward to dying, even if it should only give me restful sleep. I have no idea of what dying means, but as the days go on I seem to be standing in an open doorway, and on the side which I am still facing, all the events of my life are portrayed before me in symbolic form.

'I can see myself as a child, as a boy, as a man, and it is as if I were watching myself on a stage, when suddenly all the threads of the past gradually gather themselves together and shoot past me as one whole through the doorway in which I am standing, and into the beyond.

'What beyond? I turn round to look, and as I do so an overpowering feeling that I am about to sever my connection with earth-life comes over me. Yet I am still myself, and still, physically speaking, in bed, surrounded by those I know and love, quite conscious of pain and movement, although only dreamily interested in the remarks that are being made.

'If the doctor tells me I shall live, it will make me smile, for am I not actually standing on the threshold of real life? How can he talk of life and death like that, when he cannot know what I know? And so I turn almost with relief, and with my back to the past. face through the doorway, towards a strange country of light and life. Why have the threads of my life rushed past and left me still standing on the threshold? Why do I seem powerless to take a step forward into that strange and varied land that looks so interesting, so near and yet so far away?[1]

'Now I see . . . myself; but can that be myself?[2] That form lying there asleep among the trees by the moss-grown stream in that fair land? I am distant still, and far from that self that looks so restful; sleeping, yet so much alive. I stand waiting and wondering upon the threshold, and see those threads from the past shoot by and through me into the future, until they seem to focus upon that distant form, which is myself yet not myself. What is this mystery? And still I am in bed, and they have injected something, and I

---

[1] The threads of life referred to may have shown themselves thus to the dying man, because his life-force was passing out of his physical body into his new body, *via* the luminous cords or channels referred to earlier. These cords evidently appeared to him as a door, a long way distant.

[2] This must refer to the body or form into which he is about to pass.

am being forcibly held down. If they only knew, and would let me go! I can be of more service there to them all, when once the wrench of apparent parting is over.

'Their voices sound faint, and the room recedes. I am in bed, yes, yet I am also in that doorway—on that threshold, nearly ready, nearly. . . .

'Why, it is as if I were in pieces! No, not that, but rather as if I were extracting the real "me" from the unreal "me"; yet not that either, but as if I were rushing through myself and through myself; and through running water, rushing air, and . . . is it really me? I *must* find the door, I must, I must, I must! for it is the only door for me, the only *safe* entrance to the beyond, to that country where I can rejoin myself.

'Yes, I will go; yes, I will give up earth-life or whatever it is that I have just been through. Have I been on earth? What earth? I cannot remember. . . . There is the doorway, right ahead, and I am travelling fast, rushing towards it: the one and only door for me into the beyond.

'Am I there? It is so dim, there is the sound of rushing waters, and I only wish and pray for rest and sleep and peace. . . .

'*At this point physical "death" took place.*

('Received' some hours later.)

'The rushing waters are still about me, but I am *still*!

'Thank God for that! To rest and listen, and no longer to be afraid, to feel *safe*; it is wonderful. I cannot see the door, my door, but I *know* I am on the right side of it now,[1] and that it is closed behind me. What door? Where am I? Who was I before I found myself? Is this my real self, lying

[1] This probably refers to the snapping of the earth-cords; these cords evidently play an important part at the time of death.

so quietly here with flowers and green around me, great strong trees, and sunlight diffused into many colours everywhere?[1] The air is not air; it is colour, but *such colour*; and it keeps changing as I lie and watch it . . . changing until I can no longer fathom its mysterious beauty. . . .

'I have slept again; I am where I am, yet I am everywhere! I am myself; yet I am a self that is far greater and vaster than what I thought and felt to be myself.

'I am quite still, yet I am swiftly moving; I am neither, yet I am both. The sensation grows of the past whirling itself away into itself; yet it is here where it never was, because there is no past.

'It is stupendous; yet it is humiliation. For how dare I stir all the wonderful mechanism in and around me into motion and activity? Who was I? Where was I? Where am I now? Are these part of me? These symbols that I see before me in countless shades and lights: colour-forms, swiftly merging themselves from one great vibrating whirl into the vortex of the next?

'Are these my lives, my life, myself? . . . What mystery is this? . . . Every time I feel, or think, I quiver intensely and my surroundings change, and I lose myself and lose my surroundings, and stir up all kinds of colours, signs, and symbols. Why do I travel when I think? Cannot I think and remain myself and still? Am I yet sure that this is myself? I see, but cannot understand these forms that seem alive and flash past me. Is it speech, or the reflection of my thought, or the thought of others? God grant me rest and peace and knowledge!

[1] It is interesting to note that Major P. described this scene to his nurse some days before death and quite unknown to the present writer, who only heard of the fact some time after these notes had been set down.

'What is this? What are these flashes? Is it a sudden answer to my prayer? For I seem to *know* now who I am, or rather who it is that controls this mechanism to which I belong, which vibrates and flashes, lives and moves, and evidently is a part of me. Now I see more, and understand more; I am no longer so entirely lost within the bosom of my own extensive being.

'If I rest again and wait, it will be easier; then I will move, or rather, as I see it, make those others move to me, for I am here, and all there is can evidently be *here* for me.

'But I will sleep first, and wait and watch. All will then come my way, and I shall become all things.'

Here the fragment ended, and it became impossible to secure any further 'communication'.

PART VI

Survival: *The Interlude of Silence*

MANY research students in this field will have met with the same question that so often comes my way. It is this:

During serious illness there is often a sense of the nearness of the next world which is felt both by the patient and those around him. It is as if the two states of consciousness were approaching one another and at times even intermingling.

If, however, the illness proves 'fatal' (to use the customary phrase), then an interim period follows, during which the 'silence of the grave' descends upon those who are left behind. No longer does the next world appear to be close at hand but 'contact' seems to have been broken, followed by a vacuum or a sense of void.

This experience does not hold good where those concerned have lost all fear of 'death' and are familiar to some extent with the conditions into which we pass when we go away from life on earth. Nevertheless, the temporary void felt by the bereaved is a distressing and still far too common an experience.

Why should this be?

In my view, the explanation is both simple and consoling.

Firstly let us realise that the silence of the grave is not a negative condition but a silence filled with the qualities of healing and tranquillity.

The primary need of the soul on arrival 'over there' is to be free, free first to sleep and then to learn how to use the new form now clothing him, and to begin to under-stand the strange conditions by which he finds himself sur-rounded. For these purposes it is imperative that all emo-tional disturbances should be avoided, especially those caused by the grief, depression, regret (and sometimes fear), of those he has left behind. This is especially important in cases where belief in an after life is faint or non-existent.

It is here that Providence steps in and acting at her most merciful, screens the soul (temporarily) from all these mun-dane contacts, which could disturb or delay progress and understanding.

For those who do not realise the need for this protective screening process, what appears to be loss of contact can prove distressing. The 'Interlude' in question may last for weeks or even months of our 'time' and varies with each individual.

'Prayers for the Departed' during this period should avoid regretful thinking or attempts at communication and should be directed toward holding the loved one up in the Light and the Grace of the Creator's love. At such a time there is no better way for those who are left behind to be of real service and true help.

Very real relief is experienced so soon as it is realised that Providence knows her own business best, the result being that the 'Interlude' in question can be shortened and communion becomes possible once more. Feelings of sor-row and separation will fall into the past and love will have triumphed over 'Death' (which in any case is a Gateway and not a goal).   W.T.P.
Written in 1966

LAUS DEO